CONTENTS

KU-238-632

WATCH THE SKIES!

People have claimed to have seen mysterious objects in Earth's skies for over two thousand years. But it was not until the mid-twentieth century that the term 'Unidentified Flying Object' was first coined as a label for the phenomenon.

THE FIRST UFO SIGHTING

At 2:50 p.m., Tuesday 24th June, 1947, private pilot Kenneth Arnold was flying east toward Mount Rainier in Washington State. Suddenly, nine mysterious objects appeared in the sky before him.

They were 30 miles away, at an altitude of 10,000 feet, flying at an estimated speed of 1,200 mph, and weaving in a peculiar motion, 'like the tail of a Chinese kite'. Arnold described them as 'flat like a pie pan and somewhat bat-shaped' and 'so shiny they reflected the sun like a mirror'.

Mount Rainier in Washington State, America.

The authorities didn't believe him at first, but his story was soon backed up by other witnesses across the Midwest. Arnold quickly became known in the national press as 'The man who saw the men from Mars'.

Mount Rainier, Washington
Portland, Oregon

Kansas City, Kansas

Roswell, New Mexico

On 24th June, 1947, mysterious 'saucer-like objects' were spotted over Washington, Kansas and Oregon in America.

GRAPHIC MYSTERIES
UFOs
ALIEN ABDUCTION AND CLOSE ENCOUNTERS

by Gary Jeffrey

WITHDRAWN

BOOK HOUSE

Leeds City College

R93767

Copyright © 2006 David West Children's Books
All rights reserved. No part of this book may be reproduced in any form without
permission in writing from the publisher, except by a reviewer.

Designed and produced by
David West 🏃🏃 Children's Books
7 Princeton Court
55 Felsham Road
London SW15 1AZ

Editor: Kate Newport

Photo credits:
Page 4, NOAA; page 5, Michael Knights; page 7 (right), Lee Pettet, (left), George
Cairns; page 44 (top), European Association for Astronomy Education; page 44
(bottom), NCAR; page 45, U.S. Air Force photo by Staff Sgt Aaron D. Allmon I

First published in 2006 by **Book House**
an imprint of **The Salariya Book Company Ltd**
25 Marlborough Place, Brighton BN1 1UB

Leeds City College
Library+

PL	PW	TC	BE
☐	☐	☐	✓
☐	☐	☐	☐

Please visit the Salariya Book Company at:
www.salariya.com

HB ISBN 1 905087 81 0
PB ISBN 1 905087 82 9

Visit our website at **www.book-house.co.uk**
for free electronic versions of:
You Wouldn't Want to Be an Egyptian Mummy!
You Wouldn't Want to Be a Roman Gladiator!
Avoid joining Shackleton's Polar Expedition!

A catalogue record for this book is available from the British Library.

Printed on paper from sustainable forests.

Manufactured in China.

Soon after the first eyewitness accounts were published, the idea of the UFO as an alien controlled flying saucer became fixed in the feverish public imagination.

FLYING SAUCER FEVER!

As Arnold's story spread, other people began to report seeing flying discs all over the United States. It seemed a craze had taken hold.

The U.S. military however, remained sceptical until two weeks later, when mystery radar targets began showing up on the scopes at their secret bases near Roswell, New Mexico.

The Roswell Incident put UFOs on the world stage, and the U.S. government decided to take action. From 1947 until 1969, the United States Air Force investigated UFO sightings under a series of programmes, the most famous of which was called Project Blue Book.

Encouraged by a wave of articles and books that came out in the early 1950s, groups of civilian 'ufologists' dedicated themselves to gathering evidence about the sightings. The witnesses they found were often left feeling traumatised and disturbed by their encounters with the strange objects.

CLOSE ENCOUNTERS

Witnessing a UFO in the sky is a Close Encounter of the First Kind. Five years after the first UFO sighting, came Close Encounters of the Second and Third Kind. In these cases, a UFO or its occupants physically interact with their surroundings.

FIRST CONTACTS

On 20th November, 1952, in California's Mojave desert, the first human contact with aliens was recorded. George Adamski, a local hot dog vendor, had been hunting UFOs with six friends when he encountered a strange humanoid figure who stood approximately 1.5 metres tall. The alien was friendly and communicated with Adamski using telepathy and sign language.

A diagram of the saucer claimed to have been seen by George Adamski in 1952.

On 15th October, 1957, in Minais Gerais, Brazil, farmer Antonio Villas-Boras was working in his fields at night. Out of nowhere, a large, shiny, egg-like object landed in front of his tractor. Startled, he ran, but was caught by four helmeted humanoids in skin-tight grey overalls. He was taken aboard the craft, stripped, washed, and given blood tests.

Following the incident, Villas-Boras was deeply upset and had trouble sleeping. He was examined by a doctor who found that he had been exposed to massive amounts of radiation. These reports hinted at what would come next: a Close Encounter of the Fourth Kind . . . an alien abduction.

THE FIRST ABDUCTION

On the night of 19th September, 1961, Betty and Barney Hill were driving home through New Hampshire. What they described as a white star seemed to change into a pancake-shaped UFO. They panicked and sped away.

After this, Betty began to have recurring nightmares about horrible creatures with cat-like eyes. They also discovered that during their journey they had 'lost' two hours of time.

The couple were then persuaded to undergo hypnosis, which showed that they had been abducted by aliens and subjected to medical experiments. Many future reports of abductions would follow this pattern.

This well-known image of the 'grey' alien has evolved from many eyewitness reports gathered over the years.

Crop circles and attacks upon cattle are just some of the mysterious occurrences that have been linked to UFOs.

THE ROSWELL INCIDENT

U.S. AIR FORCE MISSILE TESTING BASE, WHITE SANDS, NEW MEXICO, 4TH JULY, 1947.

FOR THREE DAYS NOW, THE MYSTERY TARGETS HAVE BEEN FLYING OVER OUR BASES AT SPEEDS FAR BEYOND EVEN OUR FASTEST PURSUIT JETS!

DO YOU THINK THEY COULD BE RUSKIES, MR KAUFMANN?

THAT'S EXACTLY WHAT THIS GENTLEMAN FROM CIC*, IN WASHINGTON, IS HERE TO FIND OUT!

*COUNTER-INTELLIGENCE CORPS

10 P.M., THE BACK PORCH OF DAN WILMOT'S HARDWARE STORE, ROSWELL CITY, NEW MEXICO.

HONEY, THERE'S A BIG STORM STARTING UP IN THE CANYON. THERE'S GONNA BE A **FREE** FIREWORKS SHOW TONIGHT!

HEY, LOOK! A SHOOTING STAR!

NOW THAT SEEMS STRANGE... AND IT'S HEADING STRAIGHT FOR THE STORM!

MEANWHILE, OVER AT WHITE SANDS...

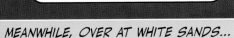

HOW FAST IS THAT TARGET MOVING?

OVER A THOUSAND MILES AN HOUR. BUT WAIT! SOMETHING'S HAPPENING!

IT'S... PULSATING!

IT'S...GONE!

BANG!

BANG!

BANG!

AAAAARRRRRGH!

KERUMPH!

CEASE FIRE!

SERGEANT! CAN WE JUST RETRIEVE THIS THING AND GET THE HECK OUT OF HERE?

YES, SIR!

OK, SHOW IS OVER! LET'S GET THIS SITE **CLEARED!**

SIR! VEHICLES ARE APPROACHING FROM THE SOUTH!

HAND ME YOUR FIELD GLASSES.

A FIRE TRUCK AND A POLICE CAR!

TAKE SOME MEN AND REINFORCE THAT PERIMETER. DON'T LET **ANYONE** THROUGH, OK?

MEANWHILE, IN THE CAB OF ROSWELL FIREMAN DAN DWYER'S FIRE TRUCK...

CAN **YOU** SEE ANYTHING YET, DAN?

JUST A BUNCH OF LIGHTS - LOOKS LIKE A DARNED CIRCUS OUT THERE!

WHAT ARE YOU?

YOU'RE NOT FROM THIS WORLD, ARE YOU?

THEN...

DEBRIS EVERYWHERE!

WHAT IS THIS STUFF?

METAL?

18

WE CAN'T LET THE TRAIL LEAD TO CORONA. THEY MUST NOT KNOW WHAT WE FOUND THERE!

SO LET'S **TELL** THE PRESS WE RECOVERED A FLYING DISC OUTSIDE **ROSWELL**...

THAT'S RIGHT! WE NEED TO STOP THIS STORY RIGHT IN ITS TRACKS.

...IT'S A STORY SO FANTASTIC THAT NOBODY WILL TAKE IT SERIOUSLY. MEANWHILE, WE CAN COMPLETELY CLEAR THE CORONA SITE!

LATER THAT DAY, ROSWELL BASE INFIRMARY.

EXCUSE ME, NURSE! COULD YOU HELP US WITH AN AUTOPSY?

SURE!

YOU'LL NEED A MASK.

GASP!

WE JUST NEED YOU TO TAKE SOME NOTES...

LATER, IN HANGAR 58.

WE'RE KEEPING MAC BRAZEL AT THE BASE UNTIL THINGS QUIET DOWN.

AT LAST! THE ROSWELL INCIDENT IS OFFICIALLY DEAD!

NOW, WE JUST HAVE TO MAKE SURE IT STAYS THAT WAY.

A FEW DAYS LATER, THE HOUSE OF DAN DWYER, ROSWELL CITY.

KNOCK! KNOCK!

SOMEONE'S AT THE DOOR! HONEY, HIDE THAT THING AND WAIT IN THE KITCHEN!

27

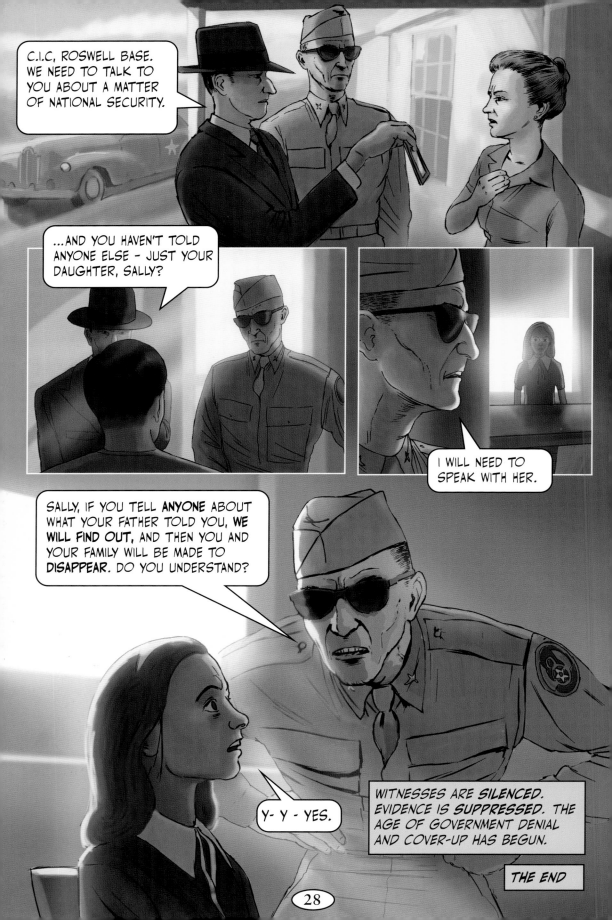

THE ABDUCTION OF TRAVIS WALTON

THE VARGINHA INVASION

19TH JANUARY, 1996, NORTH AMERICAN AEROSPACE DEFENSE COMMAND (NORAD), CHEYENNE MOUNTAIN, COLORADO, USA.

CINDACTA*, THIS IS NORAD, OUR SATELLITES HAVE ALERTED US THAT **MULTIPLE** UNIDENTIFIED TARGETS ARE HEADING YOUR WAY...

THANK YOU, WE WILL NOTIFY OUR FORCES ON THE GROUND.

*BRAZILIAN AIR DEFENSE AND AIR TRAFFIC CONTROL SYSTEM

SOON AFTER, OVER THE TOWN OF VARGINHA IN SOUTH CENTRAL BRAZIL...

AÍ MEU DEUS! LOOK AT THEM ALL!

SOME ARE FLOATING, SOME ARE SPEEDING!

WHAT ARE THEY?

MINUTES LATER...

THERE IS ANOTHER ONE OVER HERE.

SO, NOW WE HAVE THREE. THE QUESTION IS, ARE THERE ANY MORE OUT THERE?

GAAAH! THE STENCH!

3 P.M., JARDIM ANDERE DISTRICT. TWO SISTERS, LILLIANE AND VALQUIRA DA SILVA, AND THEIR FRIEND, KÂTIA XAVIER, ARE WALKING HOME, WHEN...

LILLIANE...ARE YOU OK?

WHAT IS THAT OVER THERE?

MEU DEUS!

DOCTOR, CAN YOU TELL ME HOW THIS CREATURE DIED?

I'M NOT SURE. I'VE NEVER SEEN ANYTHING LIKE THIS – I MEAN, LOOK AT ITS TONGUE...!

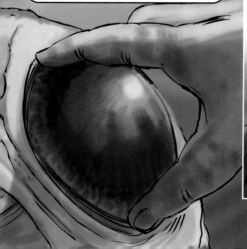

...AND THESE EYES! WHERE DID THE CREATURE COME FROM? ARE THERE ANY OTHERS?

YES, BUT THEY ARE ALL SAFELY LOCKED AWAY...

TEN WEEKS LATER, THE RESTAURANT AT VARGINHA ZOOLOGICAL GARDENS, 9 P.M., TEREZINHA CLEPF AND HER HUSBAND ARE HAVING DINNER...

...PEOPLE ARE CONVINCED THAT THE ALIENS WERE HERE! THERE IS EVEN A RUMOUR THAT A YOUNG MILITARY POLICEMAN WAS POISONED TO DEATH BY TOUCHING ONE OF THEM!

EVEN HERE, IN THIS ZOO... ODD THINGS ARE HAPPENING! SIX ANIMALS HAVE RECENTLY DIED, AND NOBODY KNOWS WHY!

ALL YOUR TALK IS MAKING ME FEEL ILL! I'M GOING OUTSIDE FOR SOME AIR.

AS SHE REACHES THE BALCONY...

GASP! I DON'T BELIEVE IT!

MRS CLEPF GOES SLOWLY BACK INSIDE. THEN SHE TURNS AROUND FOR A LAST LOOK...

...AND THE ALIEN IS STILL THERE.

43

THE END?

UFOs – FACT OR FICTION?

Are witnesses to UFOs seeing actual alien craft in the skies, or is there another explanation? Have people really encountered and been abducted by creatures from other planets, or are they imagining it?

The light from the planet Venus is often mistaken for a UFO.

MISTAKEN IDENTITY

The 1947 Kenneth Arnold sighting that started it all, has since been explained as a formation of white pelicans bathed in light reflected from snow-covered mountains.

Many alleged UFO sightings are actually the planet Venus and shooting stars (meteor events). In addition, orbiting debris from old space missions can burn up in Earth's atmosphere, causing fires in the sky. A famous incident at a U.S. airbase near Rendlesham Forest, in East Anglia, was explained as light from a local lighthouse streaming through the trees.

Lenticular (lens shaped) clouds can resemble giant flying saucers.

NATURAL PHENOMENA

Strange cloud formations (left), ball lightning, electromagnetic emissions from rocks, and temperature shifts that cause false radar emissions, have all been mistaken over the years for signs of extraterrestrial activity on earth.

GOVERNMENT SECRECY

In 1994, the United States Air Force investigation into the Roswell Incident, established that the debris discovered on the ranch in 1947 had been a top secret U.S. spy balloon, and not an alien spacecraft.

However, the heavy-handed tactics of the authorities in suppressing the true story planted a seed of mistrust with the public. Over the years this mistrust grew into outright paranoia about the government's secret involvement with UFOs. The well-known conspiracy theories involving captured spacecraft, experiments on aliens, and the use of alien technology, have their roots in the cover-up at Roswell in 1947.

RECOVERED MEMORIES

A shared feature of many alien abduction cases is memory loss by the abductee after the event. Starting with

In the 1990s, people began seeing black, diamond-shaped UFOs. Could some of these sightings have been of the then top secret Stealth fighter undergoing test flights?

the Hills, nearly all victims have needed to have their experiences recovered under hypnosis. This has led sceptics to question the reliability of their testimonies. Travis Walton's case was further weakened by his acceptance of a $5,000 payment from a tabloid newspaper for supplying evidence of extraterrestrial activity.

At the present time, while some objects in the sky may be unidentified, they are not likely to be craft from outer space.

GLOSSARY

abduction When a person is taken somewhere illegally and against their will.

affirmative An expression used to confirm the previous statement or command.

autopsy A medical examination of a body carried out after death.

canyon A deep narrow valley with very steep sides.

cargo The contents of a plane, ship, train or truck.

civilian An ordinary citizen who is not a member of any of the armed services.

debris The remains of something, such as an aircraft, that has broken apart or been destroyed.

"diabos" Portuguese word meaning "devil".

extraterrestrial A being that originated and exists outside of Earth's atmosphere.

fragment A small piece of something that is incomplete or broken.

generator A machine that provides electrical energy.

hangar An enclosed area for repairing and storing aircraft.

hoax A trick that makes people believe in the reality of something that is fake.

infirmary Another word for a hospital.

intelligence Information or evidence concerning a possible enemy.

"Meu Deus" Portuguese saying used to express surprise. In English it means "My God!"

military Relating to the armed services or their personnel.

mortuary A building or room where dead bodies are kept until burial or cremation.

mutant Living thing with different biology to the rest of its species.

perimeter A boundary that marks off and protects an area.

phenomenon An unusual event, observed through one's senses.

platoon One part of a military unit or company.

pupil The opening in the middle of an eye that appears to be black.

radar A way to detect objects and their positions using radio waves.

radiation Energy transmitted through waves.

retrieve To find and bring something back.

ruskie A negative nickname for Russians used by Americans during the Cold War.

satellites Communication devices that orbit Earth.

sentry A soldier that guards a particular post.

stench A strong, unpleasant smell.

suppress To put something down with force or to keep it secret.

telepathy A wordless exchange of thoughts.

unidentified Unable to be labelled or classified.

FOR MORE INFORMATION

ORGANISATIONS

International UFO Museum and Research Centre
Roswell, New Mexico
114 North Main Street
Roswell, NM 88203
Web site: http://www.iufomrc.com

FOR FURTHER READING
If you liked this book, you might also want to try:

Guide to the Unexplained
by J. Levy, DK 2002

The Mammoth Book of UFOs
by Lynn Picknett, Constable Publishers 2001

Atlantis and Other Lost Cities
by Rob Shone, Book House 2006

The UFO Hunter's Handbook
by Caroline Tiger, Price Stern Sloan 2001

UFOs
by Caroline Young, Usborne 1997

INDEX

Web Sites

Due to the changing nature of Internet links, the Salariya Book Company has developed an online list of Web sites related to the subject of this book. This site is updated regularly. Please use this link to access the list:
http://www.book-house.co.uk/grmy/ufos